WOKENESS IS WRONG

A TREND DEBUNKED

Tarl Warwick
2023

COPYRIGHT AND DISCLAIMER

FOREWORD

Adherents of wokeness simultaneously proclaim that it is defined, and yet undefined, that it is helpful, yet unhelpful- indeed, the terminology comes with a bit of infighting among the political bloc most likely to engage with and endorse the concept (more or less)- namely, proponents of things like Critical Race Theory- which I have treated separately in my own work "Critical Race Theory Debunked"- which has received significant praise: It was a fairly simple work because the concept of CRT is itself also simple, although it is continuously expanded, deflated, and morphed from sub-meaning to sub-meaning as its proponents attempt to defend it from criticism and expand its role at both the social and legal level.

"Wokeness" is more difficult. Some of its proponents describe it singularly as being aware of racial injustices- but that is only one puristic notion behind the term itself; it is, at least in practice, much more broad, and as amorphous (deliberately) as Critical Race Theory, which is counterpart to wokeness itself.

When we consider the meaning of words (linguistics is fun!) we have to consider what they represent, and what they represent can change, or be interpreted differently by different people. In this sense, the different definitions of wokeness are all fundamentally useful- if not wokeness itself! But when we define things for the reason of debate and discourse, it is sensible, nay, necessary, to have a solid definition in order to either reasonably support or criticize the ideal, thing, person, etc.

If I ask the reader to envision what an apple is, they will give different definitions. One will say a tasty fruit. But what of apples which are rotten? Most people do not consider those tasty. Another will say "a red, tree-growing fruit with a hard core and sweet flesh." But what of a green apple? What is a tree? Could we not feasibly consider it a bush as well, depending on size? Dwarf apple trees are not remarkably large, after all.

We can, therefore, nitpick all day, getting lost in the weeds- and this is perfectly fine for non-contentious topics. People may debate whether they like apples, but it has no real bearing on the lives and conditions of lives for people; perhaps it is a debate best left to eccentric culinary students and botanists. The two are a great example- ask a botanist and a chef the difference between fruits and vegetables and you can spend all day watching the culminating discussion.

But wokeness, being tied in directly with sociopolitics- a discourse affecting law, justice, and even economics- is therefore much more important, and it is a debate that continues. Although I consider wokeness easily defined and rebuked for its nonsense, a pretense of its proponents pretends otherwise, and hapless critics get drawn off of the debate by linguistic phantasms and constantly shifting definitions and re-definitions. To define wokeness, first we will look under the banner of *pragmatism* and *colloquial usage* at what its professed proponents and supporters subjugate to the concept to be defined:

First, that equality is a negative thing and leads to injustice- a direct tie-in to Marxist-derived Critical Race Theory.

Second; that meritocracy is also a negative force in the world, leading to inequality- which will of course be criticized when compared to its first basic tenet.

Third; Science is malleable, and there is *no absolute truth of any sort*. Except, of course, the need for wokeness.

Fourth, that all things must necessarily be subjugated to social justice (social experimentation) and centralized attempts at creating “equity”, no matter how concrete and non-abstract.

Fifth; Free speech is a form of violence.

Sixth; Tolerance should be inverted. To tolerate that which is labeled intolerance is itself intolerance, and to be intolerant is a form of tolerance when applied properly.

Seventh; Business should be subjected to sociopolitics, and *can be benevolent.*

Eighth; Marxism is fundamentally justified, if not the actions of Marxist regimes (which are normally argued not to have been Marxist by these same proponents.)

Ninth; History must be sanitized for the purpose of protecting peoples' sensibilities.

Tenth; Corporations are made sanitary through participation in ESG and similar things- even if their behavior abroad is in direct contravention to social justice.

Eleventh; Cancel culture is good, but the real cancel culture is any form of pushback against any woke policies or figures. Any criticism of them is censorship, while censorship of any other group or individual is justified.

Twelfth; The rule of law is both meaningless and even problematic.

Thirteenth and finally; everything can be racist except for actual racism, everything sexist except for actual sexism, and so forth; a Marxist style newspeak elaboration on fundamentally Stalinized tactics of yesteryear.

I will proceed to elaborate on the thirteen main tenets of wokeness and derive from that a deduction on the topic.

I: EQUALITY IS FUNDAMENTALLY BAD

Critical Race Theory- which is a subjugate component of wokeness as a broader amalgamation of social ideals and movements- teaches expressly and explicitly that equality as it is currently understood is a negative concept- or at least an unhelpful one. It proclaims this against the theoretical backdrop of equality not uplifting the historically aggrieved, which are always seen as aggregated groups instead of paying mind to individual circumstances. Thus, under this premise, Americans who have black skin, for example, are held back (as an aggregate) in terms of wealth and political power, due to historical wrongs done to them. Forsaking the premise of the Civil Rights era, and the concept that people ought to be treated equally, CRT instead proposes treating them *unequally* in order to correct for these prior wrongings. So a group perceived of as being aggrieved on an aggregate level should not be treated the same as one which is not perceived of such, but should be treated in a superior manner, in order to, oddly, equalize the equation.

This gives rise to such practices as affirmative action, hiring quotas (a de facto rule in the era of ESG, an acronym for "Environmental, Social, and Governance) and other offshoots. We may see them as leaves on a plant. The plant is singular and the leaves subjugate components.

Equity is effectively the concept of fairness in application within a system, whereas equality is more the concept of the standardization and leveling of treatment of the systems components. We can shorthand the difference between the two and say that equality is equality in practice, and equity is equality in theory only.

Under an equitable system, therefore, for example, someone whose parents were black and existed under segregation should be given some form of compensation for being held back because their parents lacked as much opportunity as their white counterparts.

This is a sham by Marxists. The concept is self evidently flawed, and the application to aggregated groups (race, gender, etc) is more about establishing voting blocs and ideological echo chambers than about any form of justice. We know this because individual circumstances are utterly ignored in the equation- a black person whose ancestors came from a state without slavery or segregation, and whose parents were both doctors, and who was born in the upper class, is perceived of as aggrieved simply because of their skin color- not because of any actual impact on their personal circumstances, or even those of their ancestors. A white person from coal country whose parents were high school dropouts and whose grandparents were respectively the town drunk, the town prostitute, and a couple of hobo itinerants, is *not* perceived of as aggrieved or deserving of any special treatment under the supposedly equitable system proposed by the woke. And this is only the racial component.

The amusing irony here is that Marxism lost round one with the civilized world predominantly because of its fixation on equity within a socioeconomic construct within which such identities and backgrounds played little if any role. Critical Race Theory, for example, I have explained, is merely communism in which the hypothetical class struggle has been redacted in favor of a hypothetical struggle based on identities and group memberships which, almost always, are artificially contrived by communists and their allies, for the purposes of promoting their ideological system which, I suspect, is geared (behind the scenes) towards returning the world to a class struggle *modus operandi*- that is, that the animus and strife caused by wokeness is effectively meant to eventually cause a jaded population to swing pendulum-like back to a class struggle, and back into the hands of economic Marxism. This is, of course, solely my theory.

II: MERITOCRACY IS BAD

Wokeness carries an element of disdain for the concept of meritocracy- a truly puristic meritocracy is one in which roles (regardless of form and function) are filled according to the ability of individuals to perform them. A persons' form of employ is a role. The ability to do some physical thing at a certain time is a role. When individuals get together in relationships we might consider those similarly. In some cases, roles are malleable and abstract (for example, two people may have different tastes regarding a certain food- the chef being merited to cook their food is largely dependent on the taste of the customer) while other roles are not- for example, there is no wiggle room, no margin of error, when calculating the trajectory of a rocket, the truthfulness and faithfulness of tax calculations, or how much to lower the fuel rods in a nuclear reactor.

Wokeness sees this latter grouping as problematic, and devises that especially forms of education and employ should be fiddled with, in order to deliver what the woke term "justice." I reject this concept on a similarly easily understood basis to the repudiation of the idea that equality is harmful or negative.

Affirmative action within education is perhaps the best potential example of woke meddling in what would otherwise at least generally be a meritocratic system. It is fairly self evident the harm that is done by this educational premise; people who are qualified for skilled work are potentially prevented from doing that work because others artificially jump the line ahead of them based solely on their skin color, gender, or socioeconomic background. Those who jump the line are similarly harmed (although this concept gets little attention!) As people are placed in employment roles, and so forth, which they are not qualified for, inevitably experiencing more difficulty with upward mobility once they enter the marginally more-meritocratic corporate construct.

The woke adjust for this concept by attempting to inject the same concept into the job site. That the business tends to promote people because of their performance is seen as problematic to the woke, and so is taken as evidence that the job site is racist or misogynistic- this is not actually the case; in large part the phenomenon can be explained by wokeness itself at the educational level. I have seen pitifully few people address this elephant in the room, either out of fear of being called "bigoted" (which is ironic) or because they have not deduced this all-too-obvious and self evident fact.

In this way wokeness shows its socialistic origins. The concept of the meritocratic structure is weakened and eventually abandoned in the form of appeasing a howling mob of people whose entire existence revolves around pretending to be outraged at "injustice"- and pretense it normally is, for the aggrieved parties are rather scant in voicing the grievance, as others do it on their behalf, speaking for the downtrodden while rather often coming from relatively comfortable college-educated and normally largely white backgrounds- and white people, wokeness argues, cannot be an aggrieved party. This is compensated for by the ever present excuse of trying to uplift others while actually helping to strangulate them.

This same bigoted woke construct for example acts in a reductionist manner, depriving all individual achievement away from, say, a black student with a 4.0 GPA who managed to grab up a masters' degree in bioengineering from an Ivy league school- a deprivation in which those who criticize wokeness all too often assume that individual was gifted their position solely because of affirmative action- the woke agree, and staunchly defend, oddly, the same basic position. There is no methodology within this framework by which the black student can individually claim merit- on the one hand because of people who refuse to acknowledge it, and on the other because of the rest who do the same for different reasons.

III: SCIENCE AS MALLEABLE

Wokeness teaches that basic, rudimentary science is malleable and should be subjugated to the social sciences. The latter point is the meaningful one; for it seeks to subjugate the absolute and objective to the debatable and subjective. This is the only realistic methodology available for the woke, for the Marxist, to interpret cold-hard data in any way other than its normally objective.

For example; wokeness would propose that the dichotomous nature of gender is to be subjugated to the social understanding of gender which it itself has concocted. The presence or absence of a Y chromosome within a human genome (which is an absolute) is therefore rendered of lesser importance than the persons' psychological expression of gender roles; which are very often hyperbolic. The law, then, should be structured not after the absolute value (the chromosome, which can easily be determined and which is an absolute dichotomy) but after the subjective value. Because the subjective value is malleable and intangible, and can be literally anything, it is helpful to the Marxist- any particular sub-ideological grouping when under attack by critics can shift chameleon-like and instantly, and the gaslighting of the critic can continue. The pragmatic arguments made are meaningless as they can always be side-stepped.

There are legitimate instances of malleability in science; for example, competing theories regarding hominid development, or the usefulness of some medicine for some purpose or another. What is of specific import here is that non-debatable points of fact which are observable, are combated when necessary by the woke, by side-stepping the objective in favor of a secondary argument, which is itself subjugate, but is presented as the higher point, subjugating in turn the more concrete understanding.

IV: FREE SPEECH IS VIOLENCE, VIOLENCE IS FREE SPEECH

One facet of wokeness is the inversion of the concept of speech and action.

The woke posit that free speech (that is, speech that offends sensibility) is a form of violence. One can also see that they often endorse *actual* violence when used for some ideological cause which they themselves support. "Hate speech" (which is legally undefined under US code and poorly defined elsewhere) is therefore *verboten*, while even violence itself is excused in the commission of promoting or defending that which is woke. This double-sided hypocrisy is self refuting and self evident; although this does not seem to phase the woke. A riot, therefore, in the name of some vacuous and vague definition of "justice" is merited, while even the most peaceable of protests, or even pedestrian speech on the internet not involving actual people interacting at all, must be policed with all vigor.

We see that this concept of justice and of speech is actually promoted by the legacy media- a term loosely relating to propagandistic media corporations, although technically it refers to any press group which existed prior to the rise of the "dot com" era. Examples cannot be given here for legal reasons, since the legal system has been weaponized by the woke; and even when the subject of scrutiny is not, themselves, woke at all, they are often browbeaten into being brought to heel by the lynch mobs which leftism spawns. An intelligent reader should be able to find ample examples on their own.

So to simply walk down the road putting out fires while happening to be armed is a form of violence- it is violence even when the violence is perpetrated initially by a mob of woke people "protesting" for "justice." Meanwhile, a small child shot by left wing rioters who are blocking traffic illegally is ignored; it may not be consciously justified (for who would justify it?) but it is buried in the media, and any mention of the phenomenon is countered with whataboutism, gaslighting, and outright lies.

That speech is speech and violence is violence is fairly key to US legal code. Speech is effectively unrestricted in the United States, unless it credibly leads to some criminal act. Nonetheless, actual violence often goes unpunished by politically motivated (or frightened and cowardly) prosecutors while speech which is absolutely legal is often at least legally scrutinized by the same, whipped on by a frenzied mob of woke leftists.

The woke, then, believe that a person offending them in any manner is somehow violating their human rights, and committing a bona fide crime, while a person actually committing a crime is excusable- so long as it is for the “right” cause. Indeed, the deliberate inversion of speech and action is nothing less than an attempt to nullify the rule of law by making the laws' application subjugate to situation and the nuance of what is or is not “justice” or what is “right”- which of course is a concept engineered by none other than the subversive masters of the lemming-like mob of wokeness.

V: ACTUAL VIOLENCE AS JUSTIFIED

Having already spoken about the deliberate inversion of speech and action little needs be said about actual violence; the woke envision it as a means to secure justice. Burning down businesses is bizarrely and fantastically claimed to be a method by which the downtrodden can be uplifted.

The basic concept would be stupid under any reasonable circumstances, but the core woke are not reasonable, rational individuals- shielded by politically motivated prosecutors and a sympathetic, aging liberal corpus, their violent actions actually *are* justified- or at least that is how the system tends to treat them. Even fairly egregious crimes result in a slap on the wrist at most- a short jail sentence, community service, perhaps a fine. It is not the woke themselves that we must blame for this particular foible- rather, a sick, highly discretionary legal system which has been subsumed by the ultra-rich should be blamed. The woke act as their pawns, fed propaganda night and day, told that they are making some sort of change in the world and that all those who stand in the way of said change are reactionary, authoritarian, evil, and condemned to the past. That this methodology is, itself, promoted fairly openly by evil and authoritarian individuals is a subject which the woke cannot seemingly comprehend.

Aggregates instead of individuals is the name of the woke game in this particular phenomenon; it is justified, they claim, to punch a police officer- even though the officer might also be woke. It is unjustified for a business owner- who might have struggled and been actually aggrieved for years or decades- to defend their business against rioters, even if the rioters have more "privilege" (to use the mythological term employed by leftists) than the business owner does.

VI: TOLERANCE IS INVERTED

To tolerate the intolerant is intolerance. To be intolerant towards the intolerant is tolerance. This is a screed of wokeness.

The logical flaw in this schema is fairly self evident to those with a functioning cerebral cortex, and therefore the concept is mostly presented with a facade of indignant self righteousness overlapped- the premise is only able to be defended by countering any criticism of the strange notion with "if you disagree, you are a bigot" or something functionally similar.

So then, tactics employed, for example, by the NSDAP in the 1940s, are utilized to fight groups associated with similar ideologies, even though the actual form and function of the tactics used, or promoted, by the woke, are more functionally similar. We see a strange inverted reality then, in which groups claiming to "fight Nazis" are using Nazi tactics against people merely gathering or speaking for some purpose simply *labeled* hateful- it doesn't matter if the gathering or speech is genuinely hateful in nature- the labeling itself is enough. Tactics such as censorship (whether by a state or corporation), the usage of the "hecklers' veto", property damage, intimidation, assault, arson. These are the hallmarks of *authoritarian* movements in general and have been for a very long time- but the woke, which engage in such behavior, make the specious claim that they are actually *fighting* authoritarianism. It is in the actual *functions* of a mechanism that we can fully understand it beyond malleable labels- and when we observe the gears, valves, and cranks, which comprise wokeness, we see, simply, authoritarianism with its hydra-like many heads. When we see those fought by the woke, we often see people with views which under no rational system would be considered problematic at all.

VII: BUSINESS SHOULD BE SUBJUGATE TO SOCIOPOLITICAL ANGLES

The woke seek to tame the wild beast which is the corporation, by injecting corporations with thoughts of "justice" and "responsibility." That this is no more than the doppelganger of business practice from the early nuclear era (injecting them with "patriotism") while the actual business structure remains identical is notable- and here I will refute the concept of businesses as social leaders not from an objective backdrop, but merely with sensible opinion and historical precedent.

We might well see the current "woke" corporate construct as twofold. It fools the small minds of the self professedly woke into consuming corporate products, while it simultaneously impacts the corporation, letting them spend a pittance on pretending to be interested in "justice." This is not demonstrably different from corporations slapping an eagle or the US flag on their products fifty years ago. Often this smokescreen doesn't originate with wokeness itself- it is a cheap corporate smokescreen, something I have actually touched on in the past with regards to a somewhat different issue- namely, moral panics.

A moral panic typically begins with a state or other empowered entity, is then taken up by "activists" who genuinely believe in the perceived threat to society, or religion, or culture, and is further perpetuated by a mob mentality among a low-info population which unquestioningly believes what they are told by the former groups. The panic extends, spreads, expands, and becomes untenable- corporate power (insofar as it did not spawn the panic initially) bows in obeisance to the cultural panic, and those who question the entire thing are ridiculed and castigated by society as pariahs. It *does not matter* what villainous group or idea is being targeted. In the end, money grubbing charlatans latch onto the panic like parasites and leech it, and it eventually attacks its own creators, after which they quietly retire their grab for power and money. Vindicated skeptics are rewarded only long after the panic ends.

This is a doppelganger of wokeness. The concept was constructed as a form of propaganda by Marxists and East-bloc subversives both at the state and non-state level. Western socialists have perpetuated it for political reasons. Corporations now bow before it in obeisance, both to prevent themselves from being attacked, and to show their fealty to the hegemonic cultural norm of the people speaking the loudest- for the silent skeptic does not complain loudly enough to bother the corporation, and there are always a few hold-outs to pacify them and cater to them, grifting in an equal manner. The rest will play out as it always has- a thesis-antithesis-synthesis in which the Marxists inject some of their ideas into society, and in which corporations make money pretending that they can actually be agents of social change and don't simply adopt the facade of being interested in the same in order to compete and make money. In the end, wokeness will collapse, having served its subversive purpose, and will be retired from the board like a chess piece which has already knocked off a couple of other pieces and must be sacrificed for the next play to begin.

We see this concept even in the story of famous panics like the Salem Witch Trials- wherein the hunt ended when the victims of accusations shifted from peasant and farmer to empowered individuals within the legal system itself. This basic timeline, this premise, is nearly always ironclad.

Indeed, one might deem wokeness a *moral panic* as much as it is an ideological "movement." Businesses can only be subjugate to sociopolitical ideology when compelled by a state or by a mass movement often sponsored by one.

VIII: MARXISM JUSTIFIED

To reckon with this particular element of wokeness (indeed, of subjugate Critical Race Theory) we must first differentiate the *empowered* proponents of the concept from the *disempowered* ones. Critical Race Theory was developed by intellectually subverted professors and distributed to students before becoming a subcultural enclave. Moral panics are developed by governments or empowered non-state entities and disseminated to the public through various networks of activists and local "leaders", eventually becoming, potentially, mainstream phenomena.

This phenomenon is nothing more than the tendency of human beings to engage in self serving behavior- greed and lust for power make sense for a life form which spent hundreds of thousands of years simply obtaining food and shelter, and only a few thousand years building what we call civilization.

Wokeness writ large is a Marxist phenomenon. The people which developed its substructure are communists. That does not mean that the average disempowered proponent of wokeness is a communist- although they are promoting communism. The term itself is not used to promote it, since the term is toxic and, at least in the stringent sense, a defeated and dead ideology- in order to promote this most gainful of ideologies, its greedy proponents present wokeness as a struggle for justice, or as a struggle for equity, as opposed to a geopolitical struggle meant to weaken any civilization which has not fully succumbed to tyranny.

The disempowered promote it at times because it sounds good on paper- much as communism sounded good to the disempowered so many years ago. Much like the concept of everyone having their basic needs guaranteed (which in theory works but in practice failed entirely), the concept of people being sensitive to others, aware of historical struggle, and amenable to helping the less fortunate, on paper, is a grand idea- indeed it is with this particular bent with which wokeness is presented. It is typically defined by its downriver proponents as "awareness of historical wrongs" or "an attempt to correct for grievances to guarantee greater equality" or something along those lines.

But because wokeness forsakes the present, real-world reality of the individual in favor of collective identity (and the collective here is no coincidence or mistake), it cannot ever actually accomplish what it seeks to accomplish according to the definition given to it by the disempowered proponents- its goal rather is to con them into believing such things will be attained by implementing its various sub-ideological principles; principles which lead to tyranny, centralized control, and propaganda, rather than to a more friendly, peaceable world.

It is indeed the more modernized, culturally appropriate variant of communist ideology, retooled for a new generation. Class struggle does not go over well with people raised in cultures which are at least marginally capitalistic- and while a handful of extreme economic leftists continue to rail against capitalism writ large, most Western leftists embrace it- or at least elements of it- and so Marxist ideology at the core of wokeness needed to be painted over with a facade- a facade hiding its true nature- otherwise nobody would adopt it.

The leaders of wokeness are the money grubbing corporation, the power grubbing post-nationalist state, and the self serving, inauthentic "activist"-in-name. All other proponents have been fooled by propaganda, and are not aware that their ideological leaders want their money, their votes, and in the end, to eliminate their democratic participation in society insofar as they can, in favor of a permanently stagnated political system in which all parties share the same broad overarching ideology... communism and fascism.

IX: HISTORY SANITIZED, AND WHY

Purveyors of the woke have continuously attempted to sanitize history (and historical monuments and literature) in the name of sensitivity- this is usually accomplished through pressure on corporations or local or state governments. The claim is that this sanitation (or Stalinization) will make the world a better, more equitable place to be.

This is not actually the case; the purpose behind such moves is clear; to deprive the public of any remembrance of ideas or ideals counter to their current narrative. The public tends to dwell even on important topics for a very short time, for a very short time is all the time they have to dedicate to anything not physically and socially proximate to themselves. A killing in the local community causes the people there to bolt the doors for months, while a killing a hundred miles distant causes a similar unease for a very limited time, say, a few days or a week.

The Stalinization of literature, film, monuments, and so forth, is effectively a perfect symbol of authoritarian movements writ large- the act of *forgetting*. Forced forgetfulness. It rides on the concept of being sensitive, but is really about making the public forget that a counter-narrative ever existed at all. In the Soviet era, figures which had been disavowed by the regime were airbrushed out of photographs and the edited photos presented as original and genuine. Possessing older copies of the material was illegal, or at least discouraged- and any claim that the narrative then newly-crafted was illegitimate and factually false was at the very least cause for harassment and intimidation, if not always imprisonment or death. We see this basic concept being carried out today on the internet, wherein inconvenient realty is "airbrushed" away in favor of a more sanitary, "proper" reality, which is not, actually, real in any sense at all.

This is not without good reason, to the Marxist, to the woke peddler. Reality does not tend to support communist causes! In the same manner that the old class struggle is now hidden behind a veneer of identity struggle, Soviet style censorship of basic, if not always happy, reality, is hidden behind a veneer of "not offending people."

But who cares who is offended? As a simple anecdote I find much personal offense in the applauding of Franklin Roosevelt- a bigoted, irredeemable crook who robbed millions of their livelihood by tossing them in concentration camps or through his prolonging of the great depression, largely purposefully, in order to subvert democracy- but that does not mean he should be scrubbed from the history books, and monuments to him torn down- rather they should be explained in a proper context, and elaboration upon the contemporary applause he received should be tempered with a view to the actual reality of his corruption.

Cultures which begin pulling down statues rarely seem to stop doing so. Cultures which burn books destroy themselves and intellectually stagnate- we have seen it before. The strong culture has no need of such acts. In this sense we can easily describe *wokeness as weakness*, and perhaps be done with it on that token; a glib terminology which I myself employ.

X: CORPORATIONS AS SANITIZED BY ESG

One element of wokeness is the misled belief that corporations can be sanitized by their participation in, loosely, ESG causes. I will merely point to the obvious here; putting up some solar panels on the San Francisco HQ roof doesn't offset the damage done by strip mining for semiconductor components, and putting up a rainbow flag on the US based website of a corporation does not offset the abuse of gays and lesbians in their foreign branches.

This facet is that of NIMBYism (colloquial acronym for "not in my backyard.") The corporation is reckoned to be cleansed or holy, because it goes through the motions of wokeness in a nation where it is accepted, while saying and doing absolutely nothing in its foreign holdings to make any form of inroads into promoting similar behavior. The same sports franchises- notably the NBA- which take the knee and fly the pride flag in the United States- are notably silent when their teams are in China. There, they do not speak out against abuse or injustice or environmental degradation- after all, that would be both illegal (generally), and unwise- they might lose their massive franchises and therefore a lot of money- which is the corporations' one true god.

While it is good that they are profit motivated (socialism being a cancer and profit motive being the unifying and inalienable source of cultural advancement) the hypocrisy shown by the corporation is secondary only to the stupidity of those who believe in such overtures. A pittance is paid by corporations in talking the talk, but virtually none of them- and none of them successful- ever walk the walk. Nonetheless, participating in wokeness makes them money, and in this endeavor they are inexplicably cleansed of their sins.

XI: CANCEL CULTURE CLAIMS "CANCEL CULTURE!" WHEN CRITICIZED

Showing the authoritarian and disingenuous nature of wokeness, proponents of the same deny that they have spawned what is colloquially termed a "cancel culture" (a culture of censorship, self censorship, and the dissociation of organic interest from algorithmic interest, especially digitally). This culture does, indeed, exist, as anyone who has spent any time in political debate can, themselves, witness. I have seen numerous campaigns launched by various sociopolitical factions to silence their opponents, often using corporate power, and occasionally through even more malevolent methods; such as "doxxing" (revealing personal information about people which is not public), or "swatting" (making false reports to the police, ostensibly to have a critic or ideological opponent raided by the police, which can easily result in death or injury.) The latter should result in attempted murder charges, in my opinion, but I digress.

Cancel culture at large is not a uniquely left wing or woke phenomenon; it is employed by governments, corporations, organizations, and single actors variably, and it would be nonsensical not to mention this. What woke purveyors tend to share as a trait, however, that goes beyond this unfortunate cultural practice, is engaging in said behaviors- and in attendant others- while decrying cancel culture itself, when it is aimed at them.

The government has no need to decry censorship, for it cannot be censored. In the off chance that a corporate entity silences a state actor, censorship is usually not brought up as a problem in the equation, and complaining reverts to claims of partisanship, of a business "taking sides" in some ideological debate. We see this frequently among those discussing the current conflict between Russia and Ukraine, for example. Cancel culture is only invoked in this particular case, by those which are not government officials at all, but rather sympathetic onlookers.

Corporations occasionally decry censorship- but it is uncommon. When they are deprived of a platform (and this is exceedingly rare) it normally comes as the result of the use of spam, or of scamming, or because (in the sense of internet technology) a site is using its competitor to try and increase its interest, and the host site to the behavior is tired of it. This non-competitive corporate aspect is separate from "censorship" at large as an issue or debate.

But the woke- that is, the corpus of people who have adopted the basic premise of wokeness- will simultaneously deny that "cancel culture" exists as a phenomenon, even when it is observable by anyone, while claiming that even *mere criticism* of their expressed views is, ironically, an "actual" cancel culture. They do not need to be banned from posting on a website, divested of their account by a bank, have a book they have published disavowed by a publisher, or find themselves harassed in any legal or extra-legal manner. Any mere criticism, regardless of the source, is amusingly claimed to be an attempt to "cancel" them, while actual cancellation- up to and including literal imprisonment- of those they disagree with, is deemed to be acceptable, and those proclaiming it part of a larger problem are helpfully labeled "conspiracy theorists."

This is merely an attempt to craft a dual set of rules; to protect against opponents by upholding the notion that established behavior and patterns of the misuse of legal and corporate power on the one hand is coincidental, while any mere criticism- and mere it tends to be- on the other hand, is evidence of bias within culture, fed by subversives, to try and "stop progress" or something of that general ilk. Too often those countering wokeness fall prey to this, worried that they are engaging in hypocritical "cancel culture" for merely criticizing the excesses of Marxism.

The greatest example of this phenomenon takes place in the realm of boycotts against businesses, or against services. Woke purveyors frequently engage in boycotts because they tend to be outsizedly successful when compared to other forms of protest- this behavior being both acceptable and legal. There is nothing wrong with Marxists refusing to do business with a company or entity they disagree with- to uphold the very concept of civilization, even the mentally depraved must have the right of association.

Boycotts may be paired with cancel culture but aren't really sum-and-substance a component of them, being a facet of culture for longer than the United States or even civilization in general has existed, beyond needing the basic organization of commerce for boycotts to exist at all. What is at hand here is the hypocrisy of the woke, in their summation of boycotts, their acceptability, and their usage in general.

The woke hope that their opponents will be gulled into thinking *themselves* the hypocrites by merely engaging in a behavior which is both effective and useful, because they are afraid that the majority of the population will crush their source of cash. Thus, they label all such attempts- which are voluntary and legal- as “cancel culture”, despite creating a *much broader* such culture through various means which even extend, often, to the illegal, or at least dubiously legal. Combating this hypocrisy requires that the opponent of Marxism ignore such claims and their spurious basis- for that is indeed the truth; boycotts (which are disproportionately labeled cancellation by the woke) are themselves *only a component of cancel culture when used as such as part of a broad plethora of tactics*. The boycotts themselves are a practice long predating the life of Karl Marx and do not, themselves, have anything to do with the concept. Neither, at the same time, does basic, pedestrian criticism, which censors nobody.

XII: RULE OF LAW IS MEANINGLESS OR BAD

Wokeness proposes that the basic framework of a blind legal system (one which is no respecter of persons) is a bad one, or at least unhelpful. This is effectively dovetailed with its argument (which I discussed prior) with regards to the need to replace equality with equity. In the proposed legal framework of wokeness, some groups should be treated with artificial preference, based on the past, in which both real and mythological claims of grievance have caused generational trauma, or something similar.

In order to counter wokeness, one must be honest; it is an absolute truth that the legal system in the United States and elsewhere is an unequal one, that blind justice does not fully exist, and that the so-called justice system in general tends to play favorites- but the woke misconstrue (deliberately or through ignorance) this favoritism as being predominantly based on race or gender instead of being based on the only real privilege which exists- that of power and money. An old saying which I repeat regularly goes; "the law is like a spiders' web- the flies are caught, the hornets go free." And indeed this is what we often see within the legal system and the application of criminal code. Those who have powerful friends are absolutely less likely to face significant charges and repercussions for even egregious behavior, than people who have little money, little influence, and little in the way of a network of support.

The woke ironically claim that corporate and legal power (this is also a tenet of critical race theory at large) should be used to correct for an unfair justice system; it suffices merely to point out that this same power is what made the justice system unfair and perpetuates this unfairness. Regular, average people do not build the criminal code- it is built by politicians, many of whom themselves profess wokeness.

XIII: EVERYTHING IS BIGOTED, EXCEPT ACTUAL BIGOTRY, WHICH IS FINE

The woke tend to define everything according to the collectivist system of identity polities- the individual is meaningless, and discounted- and is merely a subjugate part of a larger system. This limited thinking effectively prevents any recognition of *actual* bigotry within larger systems, in favor of only looking at collective groups as potentially aggrieved. The black business owner with three homes and a half million dollar a year salary is, therefore, part of an aggrieved collective, while the a Caucasian individual who makes minimum wage and lives with four roommates to pay rent and be able to eat, is not.

This is bigotry. Bigotry indeed *is* the collective view. Where individual circumstances and characteristics are alone considered, bigotry by definition does not exist. Wokeness rejects this concept of reality by pointing to equity over equality, stressing past grievances (both victim and perpetrator) as collective, thereby ignoring the individual circumstances of those lumped into both categories.

So then, the woke do not see calling a homeless white man "an oppressor" or "a colonizer" as a problem. They do not see it as demeaning to call a successful black leader "underprivileged." What is of greatest import here is that wokeness *is a form of bigotry* and disrespects both successful members of supposedly downtrodden groups, and unsuccessful members of supposedly privileged ones. It ignores entirely the privilege had by the legal and corporate powers it actually seeks to give even more power and wealth to.

THE DEDUCTION

If someone claims that we cannot describe a machine, but we then proceed to detail how it works in minutiae- for example, its gears, switches, valves, we can study its operation, and see its actual operation in real time, then we can describe the machine whether or not we give it a proper name. The name is effectively irrelevant, standing only to describe the function and why the machine exists. It has a specific mode of operation and a specific outcome to the same. I thus deduce the actual function of wokeness based on what it seeks to oppose. It opposes equality, merit, individual liberty, deregulated economics, and any form of cultural appreciation. It upholds collectivism, statism, and corporate power. So the final deduction is based on answering one question; *what are all of these things, which wokeness opposes, hallmarks of*?

The answer is simple. These are the hallmarks of enlightened Western civilization itself.

Wokeness is nothing more than an elaborate Marxist and arguably neofascist canard designed to weaken the fabric of civilization itself in order to usher in authoritarianism in every manner; legal, social, intellectual, and behavioral.

THE END

Made in the USA
Middletown, DE
28 July 2023

35862531R00015